POST OFFICES

by Emma Bassier

Cody Koala
An Imprint of Pop!
popbooksonline.com

abdobooks.com
Published by Pop!, a division of ABDO, PO Box 398166, Minneapolis, Minnesota 55439. Copyright © 2020 by POP, LLC. International copyrights reserved in all countries. No part of this book may be reproduced in any form without written permission from the publisher. Pop!™ is a trademark and logo of POP, LLC.

Printed in the United States of America, North Mankato, Minnesota

052019
092019

THIS BOOK CONTAINS RECYCLED MATERIALS

Cover Photo: iStockphoto
Interior Photos: iStockphoto, 1, 5, 7 (top), 7 (bottom left), 7 (bottom right), 8, 9, 11, 12, 16, 19 (bottom right), 21 (top), 21 (bottom left), 21 (bottom right); Shutterstock Images, 13, 15, 19 (top), 19 (bottom left)

Editor: Meg Gaertner
Series Designer: Jake Slavik

Library of Congress Control Number: 2018964603

Publisher's Cataloging-in-Publication Data

Names: Bassier, Emma, author.
Title: Post offices / by Emma Bassier.
Description: Minneapolis, Minnesota : Pop!, 2020 | Series: Places in my community | Includes online resources and index.
Identifiers: ISBN 9781532163517 (lib. bdg.) | ISBN 9781532164958 (ebook)
Subjects: LCSH: Postal service--Juvenile literature. | Post office buildings--Juvenile literature. | Postal facilities--Juvenile literature.
Classification: DDC 383--dc23

Hello! My name is

Cody Koala

Pop open this book and you'll find QR codes like this one, loaded with information, so you can learn even more!

Scan this code* and others like it while you read, or visit the website below to make this book pop.

popbooksonline.com/post-offices

*Scanning QR codes requires a web-enabled smart device with a QR code reader app and a camera.

Table of Contents

The Post Office

A girl enters the post office. She picks up a package. She also has a letter she wants to send. A **clerk** helps her send her mail.

clerk

Watch a video here!

A Place to Mail

The post office is a place to mail. People can send letters or packages. They can also pick mail up. People can buy boxes and **envelopes**.

Learn more here!

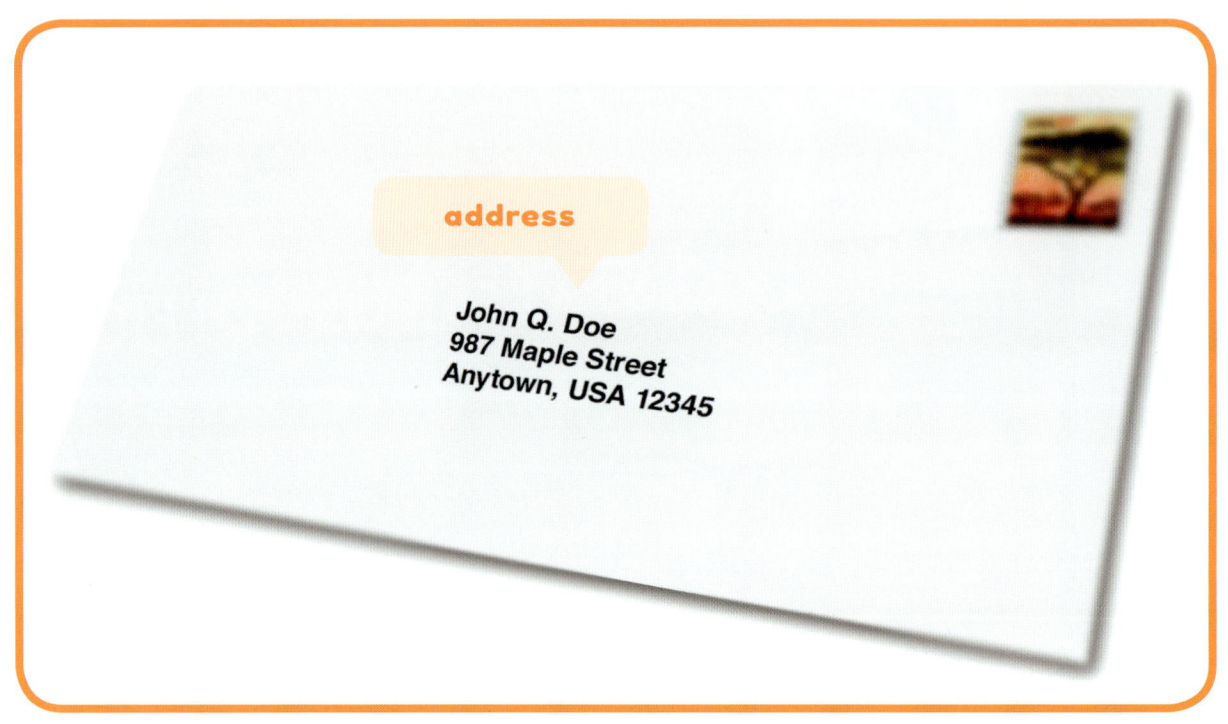

To be sent, mail needs an **address**. The address tells the post office where to send the mail.

stamp

Mail also needs a **stamp**. The stamp tells the post office the mail has been paid for.

Mail travels all around the world. Some mail goes from one state to another. Other times, mail travels from one country to another. Planes, boats, or trucks carry mail to the correct city.

Workers sort the mail.

People can pick up their mail.

They go to the post office.

Or **mail carriers** deliver the mail. They go to people's homes.

Chapter 3

Inside a Post Office

Clerks work inside a post office. People wait in line before the counter. The clerks help them send or pick up mail.

Learn more here!

The post office has many mailboxes in it. The mailboxes hold people's mail until they come to get it.

Long ago, mail was delivered by riders on horses.

The sorting room is at the back of the post office. Clerks sort letters and boxes in a big room. They make sure mail gets to the right person.

The winter holidays are the busiest time of the year for post offices.

envelopes

boxes

clerk

counter

mailboxes

sorting room

Chapter 4

Communication

Post offices are important to the community. Mail helps people **communicate**. People around the world send mail.

In the United States, more than 400 million pieces of mail are delivered every day.

Complete an activity here!

Making Connections

Text-to-Self

Have you ever gotten a letter or package in the mail? If so, what was inside?

Text-to-Text

Have you read other books about post offices or mail carriers? What did you learn?

Text-to-World

How do post offices help people communicate?

Glossary

address – the location of a place.

clerk – a person who sorts mail and helps people at a post office.

communicate – to talk, write, or share information with another person.

envelope – a folded paper that can hold a letter inside.

mail carrier – a worker who delivers mail to homes or businesses.

stamp – a sticker that pays for mail to be sent.

Index

Online Resources

popbooksonline.com

Thanks for reading this Cody Koala book!

Scan this code* and others like it in this book, or visit the website below to make this book pop!

popbooksonline.com/post-offices

*Scanning QR codes requires a web-enabled smart device with a QR code reader app and a camera.